Plants of Prey

-Text and photographs by Densey Clyne-

Gareth Stevens Publishing
MILWAUKEE

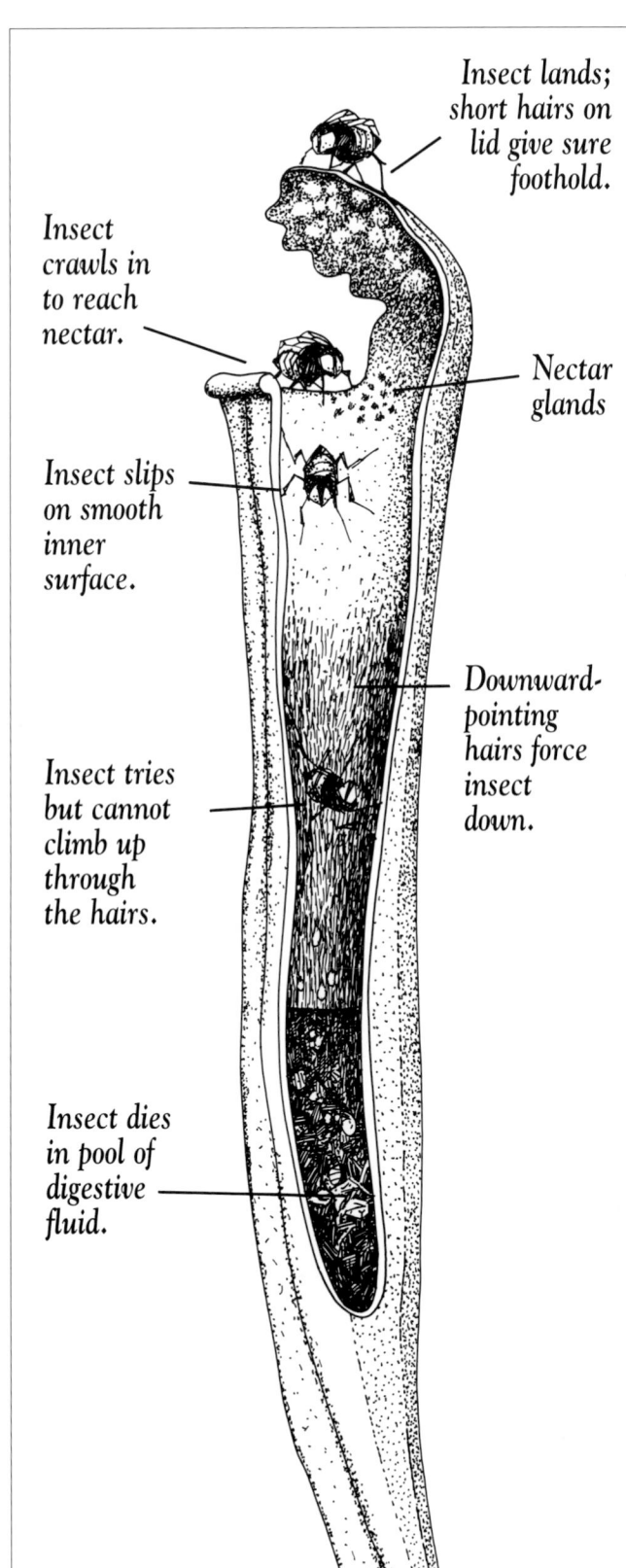

Insect lands; short hairs on lid give sure foothold.

Insect crawls in to reach nectar.

Insect slips on smooth inner surface.

Insect tries but cannot climb up through the hairs.

Insect dies in pool of digestive fluid.

Nectar glands

Downward-pointing hairs force insect down.

An insect lands on a leaf of a pitcher plant to drink **nectar**. The insect loses its balance on the slippery surface, slides down the inside of the pitcher plant, and falls into the pool of liquid at the bottom. The insect cannot fly with wet wings. It cannot climb out because hairs on the sides of the plant point down-ward, forcing it down. It's trapped and digested by the plant.

Words that appear in the glossary are printed in **boldface** type the first time they occur in the text.

Many insects eat plants, but did you know that there are also plants that eat insects? They are **carnivorous**, or **insectivorous**, plants.

The trumpet pitcher plants *(above)* are **plants of prey** found in the United States. They look harmless and pretty enough to use in a flower arrangement.

But pitcher plants are not flowers. They are leaves that are specially designed to trap insects.

Sundews

This sundew plant eats insects, but how does it catch them? Sundews attract insects by offering them something to drink.

Sundews grow in all kinds of places. They do not all look the same, but you can recognize them because the leaves are covered with tiny "dewdrops" that sparkle in the Sun. The "dew"-covered leaf (*above*) is an inviting place for a thirsty insect. But dew is simply water. If these tempting droplets were just water, the Sun would quickly dry them. These droplets gleam in the Sun even on the hottest days.

There is a good reason why sundew droplets do not dry up and disappear. They are not really dewy — they are gluey, or even gooey, and sticky! If you were a small insect, you would get stuck very quickly.

It takes an extra-strong pair of wings from an extra-strong insect to pull free from the droplets. A fly landing on this leaf has no chance of escape.

This rosetted sundew feeds on ants. It spreads its leaves close to the ground to attract them.

A tiny ant cannot pull itself free from the droplets, even with all those legs. In fact, the six legs become anchor points for the plant's sticky threads to bind the ant to the leaf.

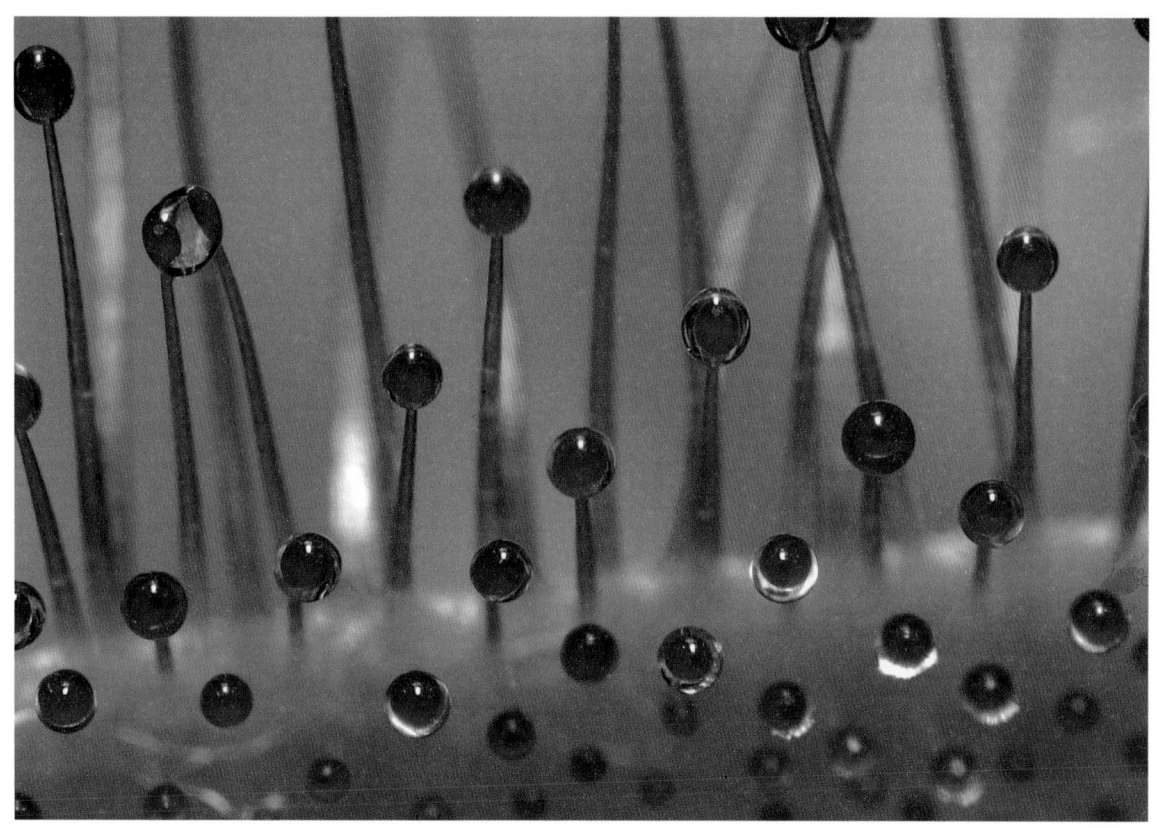

Each of the droplets on a sundew leaf sits on a stalk. At the top of each stalk, there's a knob that is visible through the clear, sticky fluid. The knobs and stalks of some sundews are bright red.

The knobs are **glands**. Plants have glands, just as people and animals do. Sundews have hundreds of them.

The glands produce the sticky fluid that turns a harmless-looking leaf into a sort of living flypaper.

Butterflies need to drink, but the thirsty one (*above*) made a terrible mistake when it landed on a sundew.

Butterflies are not powerful fliers. Their large wings only help to stick them even more firmly to the leaf.

Many tall sundews are especially attractive to flies. When a fly gets stuck, it struggles for a while, but this only makes the situation worse. It cannot escape, and eventually it dies, becoming a meal for a hungry plant.

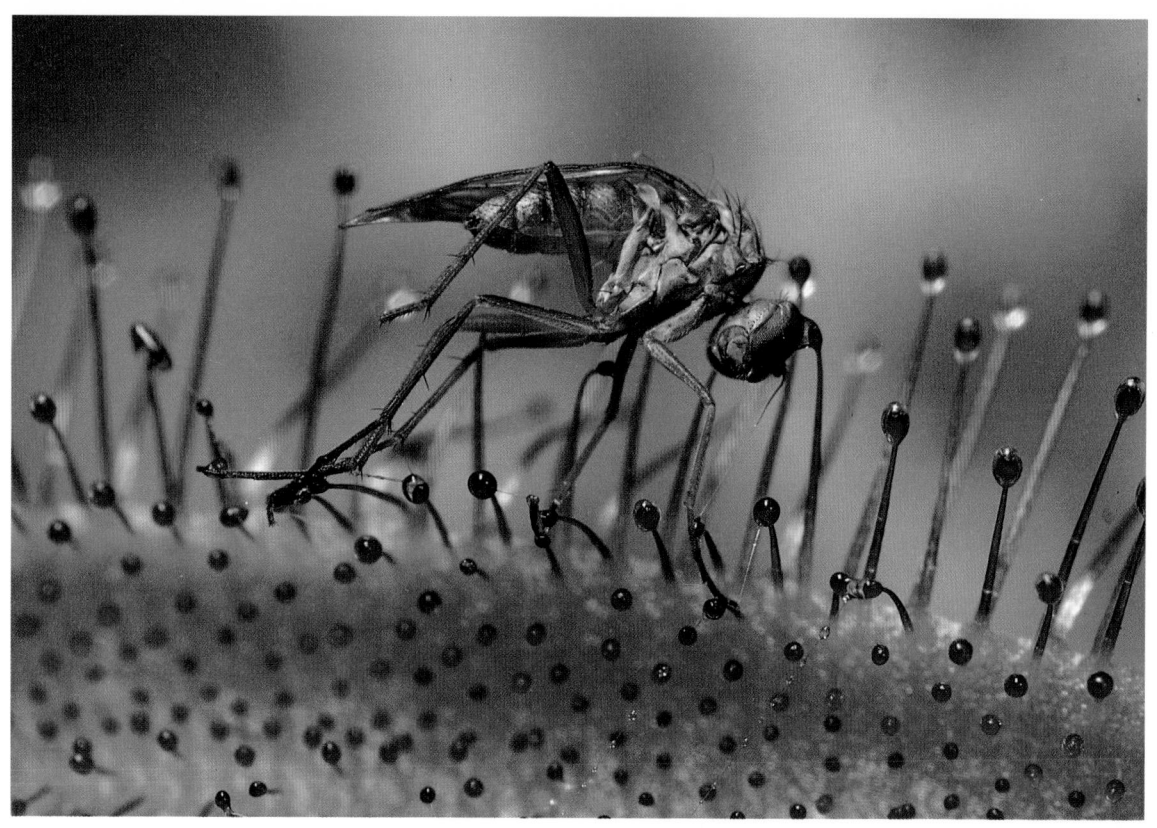

Once the plant has attracted and trapped an insect, how does it eat the meal? The sundew's droplets contain digestive **enzymes**. These enzymes slowly break down the soft parts of the insect's body and turn them into a liquid. The leaf absorbs the liquid, and the plant gets the food it needs to grow.

This is similar to what happens when people eat food. Enzymes in our mouths and stomachs break down food so our bodies can absorb it for nourishment.

Some insects outsmart the sundew. One type of bug *lives* on sundew plants! By moving carefully between the sticky drops, it gets a free meal — the other insects freshly caught by the sundew.

Like most plants, sundews produce flowers. The flowers need to be **pollinated** to produce seeds for new plants. Plants need insects to carry **pollen** from one flower to another. So even though sundews eat some insects, they have a friendly relationship with others. These insects safely visit the flowers and fly away again without getting stuck.

Pitcher plants

Like sundews, pitcher plants come in a variety of shapes. They also use their leaves to trap insects, but they do it with a slippery dip and a treacherous pool instead of sticky droplets.

The diagram on page 2 details just how dangerous this plant is to insects. An insect lands on a plant for a quick meal when suddenly the tables turn, and the plant is the one that will be having the meal.

Pitcher plants can be found in many areas of the world from jungles to mountaintops.

 Pitcher is another word for a jug or container. The leaf of a pitcher plant is similar to a jug, with smooth, steep sides and a pool of liquid at the bottom. But it is not a pool of water; it is a pool of digestive enzymes.

Around the top of each leaf are tiny glands that produce nectar — sweet food for insects.

Like sundews, pitcher plants also need to be pollinated. For this reason, they *do not harm* the insects that *do this job* for them.

The flowers are located well apart from the leaves and *do not trap* the pollinating insects.

Pitcher plants have large, noticeable flowers that contain pollen and nectar. The flower's nectar probably smells different from the nectar on the leaves, in order to attract various kinds of insects.

This pitcher plant *(below)* has short, wide pitchers. It grows low on the ground in damp, boggy places. It attracts ants as well as flying insects.

The plant grows only in Western Australia. Clearing of the land for farming has almost eliminated its **habitat**, and humans have uprooted so many plants that there are hardly any left. The plant is now protected by law, so perhaps it will be able to survive.

These pitcher plants grow in Malaysia and benefit from heat and humidity all year round. These conditions attract many insects.

This Australian-New Guinea tropical pitcher plant is a straggly climber that supports itself on taller plants. It has large pitchers that dangle at the end of long, twisted **tendrils**, or leaf-stalks. A pitcher can be any part of a plant except the flowers or roots.

This praying mantis (below) waits patiently on the lid of a tropical pitcher plant. Like the pitcher plant, the praying mantis is an insect-eater, too.

The mantis grabs insects as they land on the pitcher — before the plant has a chance to catch them.

The lid of this pitcher stays open all the time. It seems to work more like an umbrella than a close-fitting lid, keeping rainwater out of the pitcher.

Venus's-flytraps

The Venus's-flytrap grows in a few swampy areas in North and South Carolina in the United States. Its hinged leaves with spiky edges act as traps that snap shut on its **prey**. Flies and other insects may be attracted by the bright color at the center of the trap or by the scent.

Although the flytrap's leaves move fast for a plant, the movement is actually very slow, so the prey is not frightened away.

Ants, flies, moths, beetles, grasshoppers, and even worms are no match for the grip of the Venus's-flytrap.

When an insect lands on a Venus's-flytrap to look for a meal, it touches some of the hairs on the plant's leaf. The pressure on these hairs triggers the leaf to close — slowly but surely.

The leaf stays shut for several days, while the soft parts of the insect are digested.

Bladderworts

Bladderworts are small carnivorous plants that also catch their prey in traps. They live in swampy soil or in the water itself. The flowers are visible, but the traps are not.

The traps are tiny, empty bags, or **bladders**, hidden in tangled stems underground or in the water. They catch tiny creatures that live in **stagnant** water. This bladderwort (*above*) has caught a worm.

When a tiny creature brushes against sensitive bladder hairs on the plant, a trapdoor opens. It takes less than one-fiftieth of a second for the trapdoor to flip open. Water rushes in, along with the victim. The door closes, and the plant now has a meal.

Why *do* carnivorous plants eat insects when most plants *do not?* The reason is that the swampy soil and stagnant waters where carnivorous plants make their homes lack the **nutrients** that all plants need. The bodies of insects supply these nutrients.

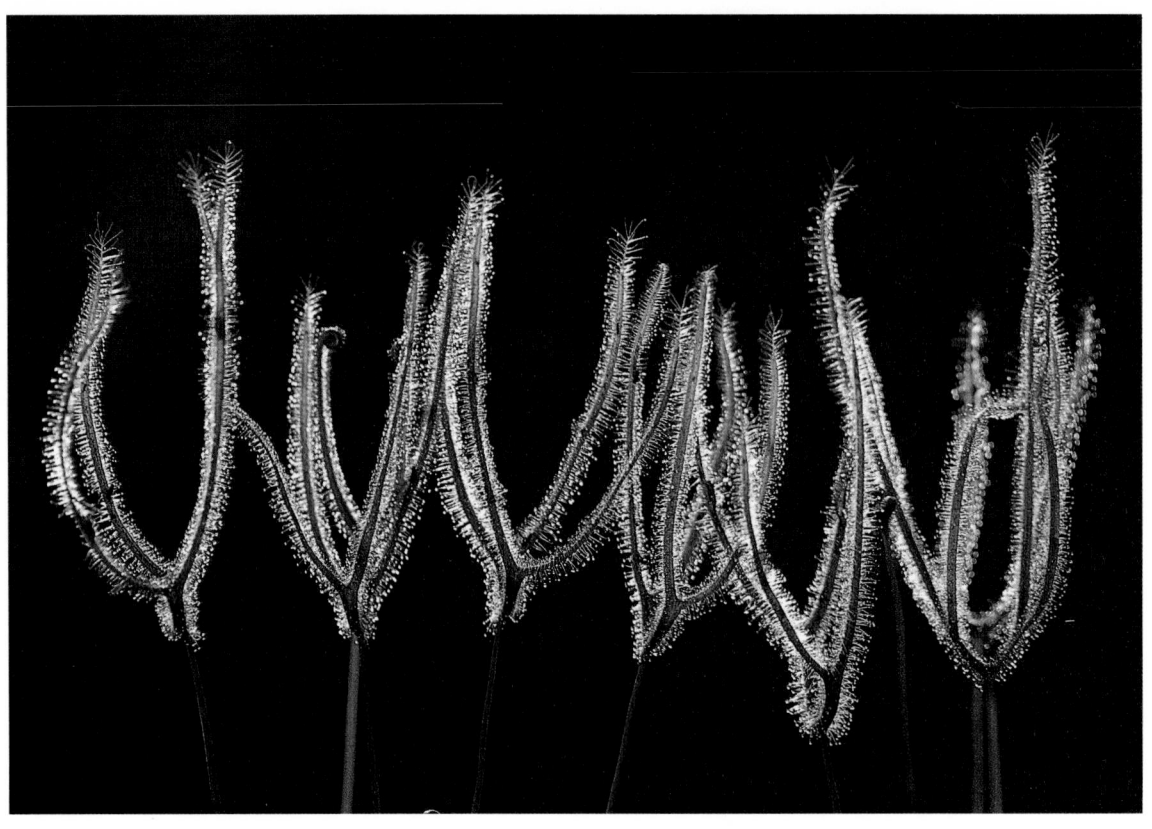

The special tricks and traps of carnivorous plants enable them to live in habitats where there is not enough food for other types of plants. So plants of prey thrive without much **competition** from other plants.

Plants of prey have **adapted** to make the most of what nature offers in habitat and food. It is important to **preserve** habitat for these plants as well as for all living beings in the wild.

Plentiful and suitable habitat is necessary whether the living beings move around or are rooted in one spot like the elegant pitcher plants (*above*).

Before it is too late, contact a conservation organization and become involved in saving our fragile environments — for all the plants and creatures of the world, including ourselves.

Glossary

adapted: changed so as to be able to survive in the existing conditions.

bladder: a springy sac or a tiny, empty bag that stores a liquid.

carnivorous: a way to describe a plant or animal that eats meat.

competition: struggling with others to survive.

enzyme: a substance produced by the body that is designed for a specific purpose.

gland: an organ in the body that manufactures special substances for accomplishing certain tasks.

habitat: the place in nature where an animal or plant lives and thrives.

insectivorous: a way to describe a plant or animal that eats insects.

nectar: the sweet liquid produced by flowers that attracts bees, birds, and other animals.

nutrient: ingredients in food that nourish a plant or animal.

plants of prey: plants that feed on insects.

pollen: tiny spores produced by plants and carried by insects from flower to flower.

pollinated: when pollen is placed on a plant to produce seeds.

preserve: to protect and save from destruction.

prey: an animal that is hunted for food by other animals.

stagnant: not moving or flowing; very still.

tendril: a thin, coiling part of a plant.

Books to Read

Bloodthirsty Plants (series). Victor Gentle (Gareth Stevens)

Carnivorous Plants. Nancy J. Nielsen (Watts)

Eco-Journey (series). Barbara J. Behm and Veronica Bonar (Gareth Stevens)

Pitcher Plants: The Elegant Insect Traps. Carol Lerner (Morrow)

The Science Book of Things That Grow. Neil Ardley (Harcourt)

Young Naturalist Field Guides (series). (Gareth Stevens)

Videos

Carnivorous Plants. (Pyramid Media)

The Importance of Plants to Our World. (United Learning)

Plants and Insects. (Films for the Humanities and Sciences)

The World of Insectivorous Plants. (Films for the Humanities and Sciences)

Web Sites

literary.com.gsinc/pages/pol.html

www.ocean.com/au/vcps/drosera.htm

www.hpl.hp.com/bot/cp_home

www.flytrap.demon.co.uk/glossary/gloss_b.htm

Index

For a free color catalog describing
Gareth Stevens Publishing's list of high-
quality books and multimedia programs,
call 1-800-542-2595 (USA) or 1-800-
461-9120 (Canada). Gareth Stevens
Publishing's Fax: (414) 225-0377.
See our catalog, too, on the World Wide
Web: http://gsinc.com

The publisher would like to extend special
thanks to Jan W. Rafert, Curator of
Primates and Small Mammals, Milwaukee
County Zoo, Milwaukee, Wisconsin, for his
kind and professional help with the
information in this book.

Library of Congress Cataloging-in-
Publication Data

Clyne, Densey.
    Plants of prey / by Densey Clyne.
      p. cm. — (Nature close-ups)
    "First published in 1992 by Allen & Unwin
Pty Ltd . . . Australia" — T.p. verso.
    Includes bibliographical references
and index.
    Summary: Reveals the world of the
ingenious, carnivorous plants that prey
on insects.
    ISBN 0-8368-2060-6 (lib. bdg.)
    1. Carnivorous plants—Juvenile literature.
[1. Carnivorous plants.] I. Title. II. Series:
Clyne, Densey. Nature close-ups.
QK917.C59   1998
583'.75—dc21   97-31735

First published in North America
in 1998 by
Gareth Stevens Publishing
1555 North RiverCenter Drive
Suite 201
Milwaukee, WI 53212 USA

First published in 1992 by Allen & Unwin
Pty Ltd, 9 Atchison Street, St. Leonards,
NSW 2065, Australia. Text and
photographs © 1992 by Densey Clyne.
Additional end matter © 1998 by
Gareth Stevens, Inc.

Printed in the United States of America

1 2 3 4 5 6 7 8 9 02 01 00 99 98